PIANO · VOCAL · GUITAR

MW00681614

CANADIAN POP/ROCK

This publication is not for sale in the EU.

ISBN 0-634-05694-8

HAL•LEONARD®
CORPORATION

7777 W. BLUEMOUND RD. P.O. BOX 13819 MILWAUKEE, WI 53213

Visit Hal Leonard Online at
www.halleonard.com

ADIA

Words and Music by SARAH McLACHLAN
and PIERRE MARCHAND

we all fal - ter. And does it mat -

- ter? __ - ter? __

BIRD ON THE WIRE
(Bird on a Wire)

Words and Music by
LEONARD COHEN

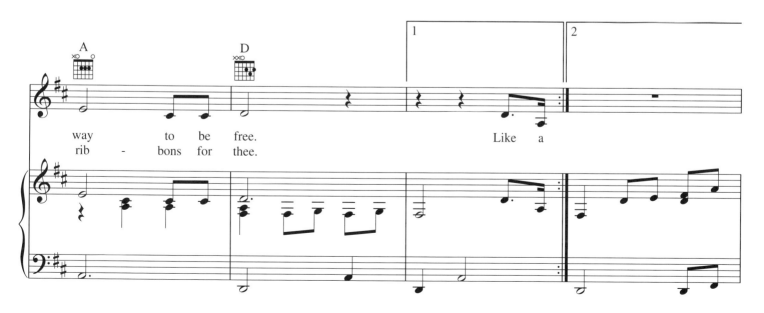

ANGEL

Words and Music by
SARAH McLACHLAN

Original key: Db major. This edition has been transposed down one half-step to be more playable.

To Coda ⊕

BLACK VELVET

Words and Music by CHRISTOPHER WARD
and DAVID TYSON

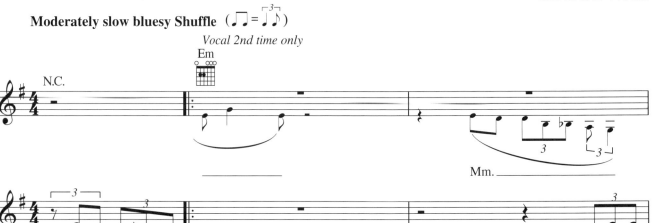

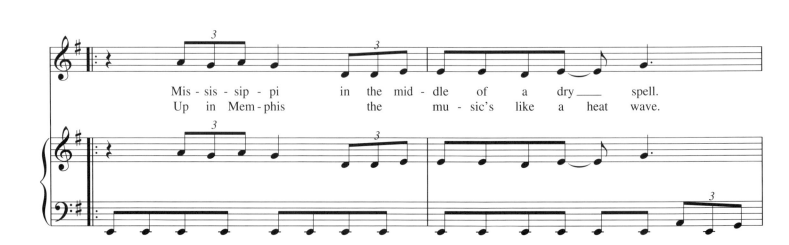

Mis - sis - sip - pi in the mid - dle of a dry___ spell.
Up in Mem - phis the mu - sic's like a heat wave.

COMPLICATED

Words and Music by AVRIL LAVIGNE, LAUREN CHRISTY,
SCOTT SPOCK and GRAHAM EDWARDS

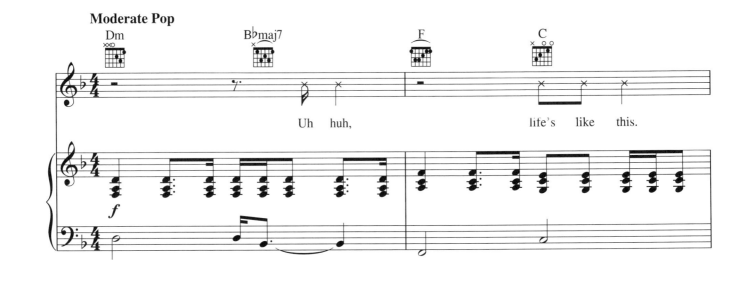

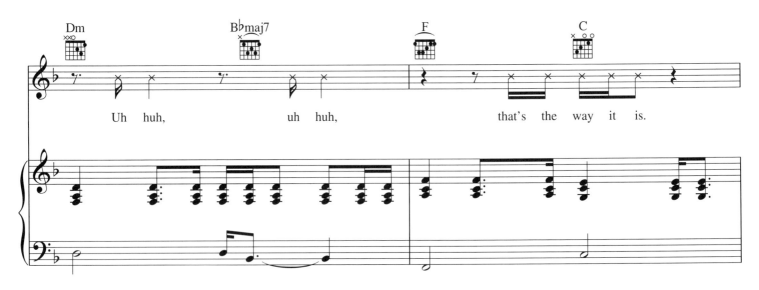

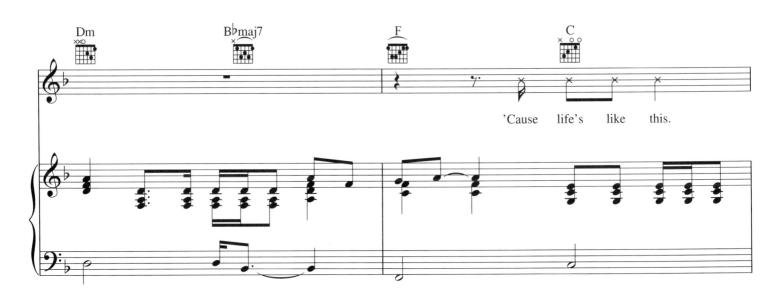

DON'T FORGET ME
(When I'm Gone)

Words and Music by SAM REID,
ALAN FREW and JIM VALLANCE

lov - ing you.___ Oh,___ can this be true.___

ev - 'ry where,___ oh,___ but you don't care.___

If ___

Don't for - get me when I'm gone,___ my

heart would break.— I have loved you for so long,—

is noth - ing wrong?

Repeat and fade

GRACE, TOO

Words and Music by ROBERT BAKER,
GORDON SINCLAIR, JOHN FAY,
PAUL LANGLOIS and GORDON DOWNIE

He said, "I'm fab-'lous-ly rich.

The se - cret rules of en - gage - ment   are hard to en - dorse

when the ap - pear - ance of con - flict

D.S. al Coda

meets the ap - pear - ance of force.

But I can guar - an - tee

CODA

E

A/E

E

E5

FAT LIP

Words and Music by
SUM 41

Storm - ing through the par - ty like my name is El Ni - no, when I'm hang - ing out drink - ing in the
know us at all, we laugh when old peo - ple fall. But what would you ex - pect with a

HAVE YOU EVER REALLY LOVED A WOMAN?

from the Motion Picture DON JUAN DeMARCO

Words and Music by BRYAN ADAMS,
MICHAEL KAMEN and ROBERT JOHN LANGE

Additional Lyrics

2. To really love a woman, let her hold you
   Till ya know how she needs to be touched.
   You've gotta breathe her, really taste her.
   Till you can feel her in your blood.
   N' when you can see your unborn children in her eyes.
   Ya know ya really love a woman.

   When you love a woman
   You tell her that she's really wanted.
   When you love a woman
   You tell her that she's the one.
   'Cause she needs somebody to tell her
   That you'll always be together
   So tell me have you ever really,
   Really really ever loved a woman.

3. *Instrumental*

   Then when you find yourself
   Lyin' helpless in her arms.
   You know you really love a woman.

   When you love a woman *etc.*

LET IT RIDE

Words and Music by RANDY BACHMAN
and CHARLES TURNER

Lyrics:
Good - bye, ___ hard life, ___
don't cry. ___ Would you let it ride? ___

You can't see the morn - in', but I can see the light. __
Babe, my life is not __ com - plete; I nev - er see you smile. __

Ride, ride, ride, let it ride. __
Ride, ride, ride, let it ride. __

While you've been out run - nin', I've __ been wait - in' half the night. __
Ba - by, you want the for - giv - in' kind __ and that's just not my style. __
I've been do - in' things worth - while __ and you've been book - in' time. __

62

say good - bye or would you let it ride?

D.S. al Coda

CODA

F#m

Would you let it ride?_

Would you let it ride?_

Would you let it ride?_

HEAVEN

Words and Music by BRYAN ADAMS
and JIM VALLANCE

MY HEART WILL GO ON
(Love Theme from 'Titanic')
from the Paramount and Twentieth Century Fox Motion Picture TITANIC

Music by JAMES HORNER
Lyric by WILL JENNINGS

Ev - 'ry night in my dreams I see you, I feel you, that is how I know you go on.

MY LAST CIGARETTE

Words and Music by MARK HEWERDINE,
GARY CLARK and NEIL MacCOLL

Some - times _____ the peo - ple who love in the night _____

SEASONS IN THE SUN
(Le Moribond)

English Lyric by ROD McKUEN
Music by JACQUES BREL

THE POWER OF THE DREAM

Words and Music by BABYFACE,
DAVID FOSTER and LINDA THOMPSON

LOVE THEME FROM ST. ELMO'S FIRE

from the Motion Picture ST. ELMO'S FIRE

Words and Music by
DAVID FOSTER

SIGN OF THE GYPSY QUEEN

Words and Music by
LORENCE HUD

Light-ning smokes on the hill____ rise;____
Get my sad-dle and tie it on____

brought the man with the warn-in' light,____
West-ern Wind, who is fast and strong.____

shout-in' loud, "You had bet-
Jump on back, he is good

Sign of the Gyp-sy Queen;_____ pack your things and leave._____

Word of a wom-an who knows:____ "Take all your gold and you go."_____

SK8ER BOI

Words and Music by AVRIL LAVIGNE, LAUREN CHRISTY,
SCOTT SPOCK and GRAHAM EDWARDS

Lively Rock

He was a boy. She was a girl. Can I make it an - y more ob - vi - ous? He was a punk. She did bal - let. What more can I say?

Lyrics:
— e - nough for her. Now he's a su - per star, slam - ming on his

gui - tar. Does your pret - ty face see what he's worth? He was a skat -

— see what he's worth?

SOMEBODY'S OUT THERE

Words and Music by MIKE LEVINE,
GIL MOORE and RIK EMMETT

Moderately fast

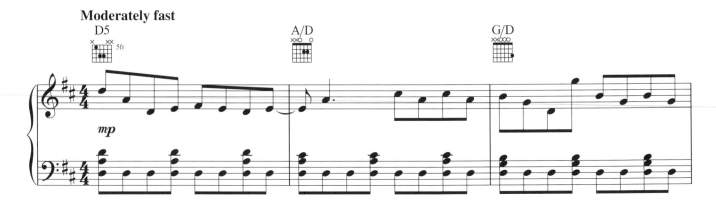

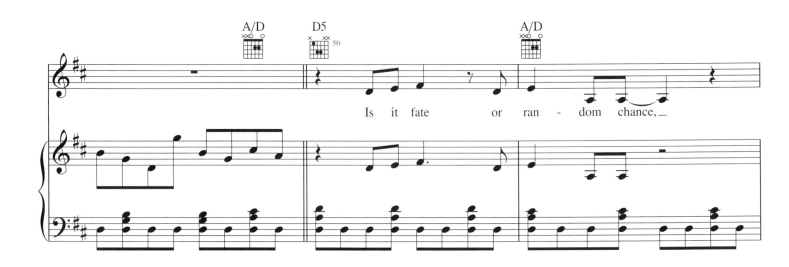

Is it fate or ran - dom chance, ___

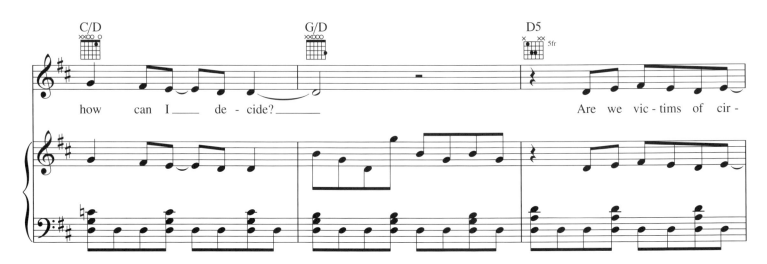

how can I ___ de - cide? ___ Are we vic - tims of cir -

TAKIN' CARE OF BUSINESS

Words and Music by
RANDY BACHMAN

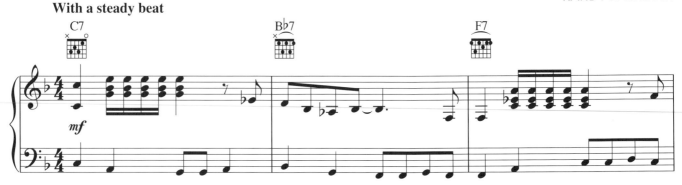

They get up ev - 'ry morn - in' from the
eas - y as fish - in', you could

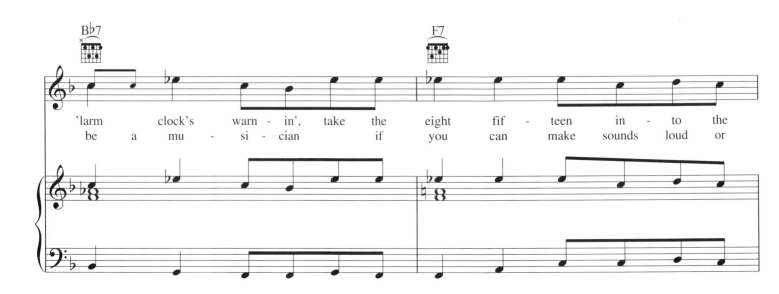

'larm clock's warn - in', take the eight fif - teen in - to the
be a mu - si - cian if you can make sounds loud or

city.
mel - low.

There's a whis - tle up a - bove and peo - ple
Get a sec - ond - hand gui - tar_____ chanc - es

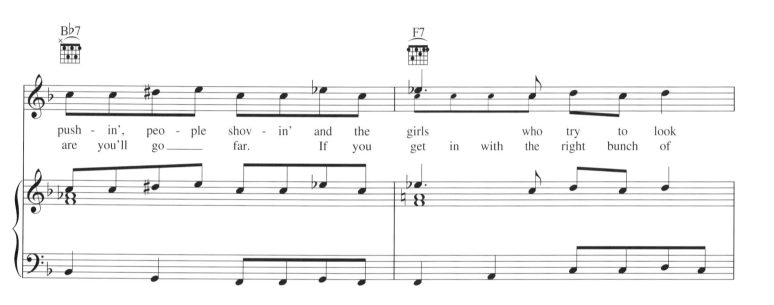

push - in', peo - ple shov - in' and the girls who try to look
are you'll go_____ far. If you get in with the right bunch of

pret - ty.
fel - lows.

And if your train's on time, you can
Peo - ple see you hav - in' fun, just a

get to work by nine, and start your slav - in' job to get your
ly - in' in the sun. Tell them that you like it this way.

pay. If you ev - er get an - noyed look at
___ It's the work that we a - void and we're

me, I'm self - em - ployed, I love to work at noth - in' all day.
all self - em - ployed. We like to work at noth - in' all day.

124

THESE EYES

Written by BURTON CUMMINGS
and RANDY BACHMAN

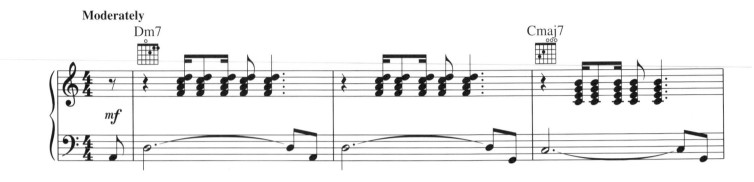

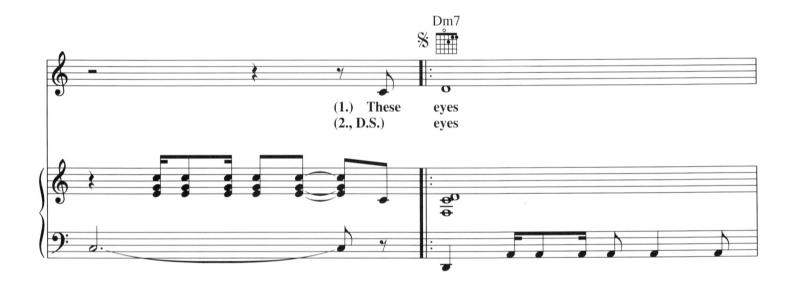

THIS COULD BE THE NIGHT

Words and Music by PAUL DEAN, MIKE RENO,
BILL WRAY and JONATHAN CAIN

D.S. al Coda

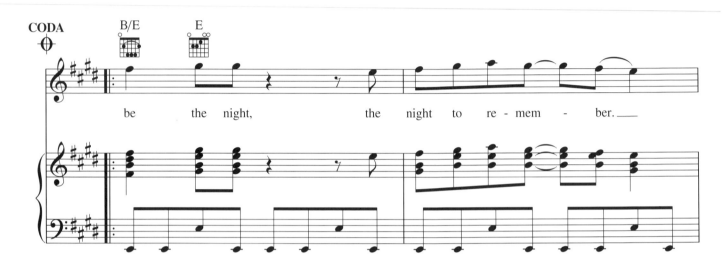

be the night, the night to re - mem - ber.____

We'll make it last____ for - ev - er. This could

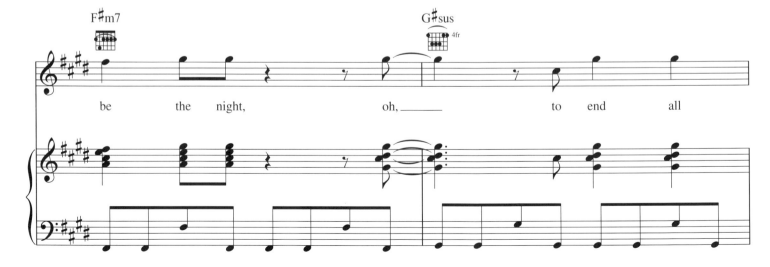

be the night, oh,____ to end all

SOMETIMES WHEN WE TOUCH

Words by DAN HILL
Music by BARRY MANN

142

Contemporary Classics

Your favorite songs for piano, voice and guitar.

The Definitive Rock 'n' Roll Collection
A classic collection of the best songs from the early rock 'n' roll years – 1955-1966. 97 songs, including: Barbara Ann • Chantilly Lace • Dream Lover • Duke of Earl • Earth Angel • Great Balls of Fire • Louie, Louie • Rock Around the Clock • Ruby Baby • Runaway • (Seven Little Girls) Sitting in the Back Seat • Stay • Surfin' U.S.A. • Wild Thing • Woolly Bully • and more.
00490195 ....$29.95

The Big Book of Rock
78 of rock's biggest hits, including: Addicted to Love • American Pie • Born to Be Wild • Cold As Ice • Dust in the Wind • Free Bird • Goodbye Yellow Brick Road • Groovin' • Hey Jude • I Love Rock 'N' Roll • Lay Down Sally • Layla • Livin' on a Prayer • Louie Louie • Maggie May • Me and Bobby McGee • Monday, Monday • Owner of a Lonely Heart • Shout • Walk This Way • We Didn't Start the Fire • You Really Got Me • and more.
00311566..$19.95

Big Book of Movie Music
Features 73 classic songs from 72 movies: Beauty and the Beast • Change the World • Eye of the Tiger • I Finally Found Someone • The John Dunbar Theme • Somewhere in Time • Stayin' Alive • Take My Breath Away • Unchained Melody • The Way You Look Tonight • You've Got a Friend in Me • Zorro's Theme • more.
00311582 ....$19.95

The Best Rock Songs Ever
70 of the best rock songs from yesterday and today, including: All Day and All of the Night • All Shook Up • Blue Suede Shoes • Born to Be Wild • Boys Are Back in Town • Every Breath You Take • Faith • Free Bird • Hey Jude • I Still Haven't Found What I'm Looking For • Livin' on a Prayer • Lola • Louie Louie • Maggie May • Money • (She's) Some Kind of Wonderful • Takin' Care of Business • Walk This Way • We Didn't Start the Fire • We Got the Beat • Wild Thing • more!
00490424 ....$18.95

Contemporary Vocal Groups
This exciting new collection includes 35 huge hits by 18 of today's best vocal groups, including 98 Degrees, TLC, Destiny's Child, Savage Garden, Boyz II Men, Dixie Chicks, 'N Sync, and more! Songs include: Bills, Bills, Bills • Bug a Boo • Diggin' on You • The Hardest Thing • I'll Make Love to You • In the Still of the Nite (I'll Remember) • Ready to Run • Tearin' Up My Heart • Truly, Madly, Deeply • Waterfalls • Wide Open Spaces • and more.
00310605 ....$14.95

Motown Anthology
This songbook commemorates Motown's 40th Anniversary with 68 songs, background information on this famous record label, and lots of photos. Songs include: ABC • Baby Love • Ben • Dancing in the Street • Easy • For Once in My Life • My Girl • Shop Around • The Tracks of My Tears • War • What's Going On • You Can't Hurry Love • and many more.
00310367 ....$19.95

Best Contemporary Ballads
Includes 35 favorites: And So It Goes • Angel • Beautiful in My Eyes • Don't Know Much • Fields of Gold • Hero • I Will Remember You • Iris • My Heart Will Go On • Tears in Heaven • Valentine • You Were Meant for Me • You'll Be in My Heart • and more.
00310583 ....$16.95

Contemporary Hits
Contains 35 favorites by artists such as Sarah McLachlan, Whitney Houston, 'N Sync, Mariah Carey, Christina Aguilera, Celine Dion, and other top stars. Songs include: Adia • Building a Mystery • The Hardest Thing • I Believe in You and Me • I Drive Myself Crazy • I'll Be • Kiss Me • My Father's Eyes • Reflection • Smooth • Torn • and more!
00310589..$16.95

Jock Rock Hits
32 stadium-shaking favorites, including: Another One Bites the Dust • The Boys Are Back in Town • Freeze-Frame • Gonna Make You Sweat (Everybody Dance Now) • I Got You (I Feel Good) • Na Na Hey Hey Kiss Him Goodbye • Rock & Roll – Part II (The Hey Song) • Shout • Tequila • We Are the Champions • We Will Rock You • Whoomp! (There It Is) • Wild Thing • and more.
00310105 ....$14.95

Rock Ballads
31 sentimental favorites, including: All for Love • Bed of Roses • Dust in the Wind • Everybody Hurts • Right Here Waiting • Tears in Heaven • and more.
00311673..$14.95

FOR MORE INFORMATION, SEE YOUR LOCAL MUSIC DEALER, OR WRITE TO:

HAL•LEONARD®
CORPORATION
7777 W. BLUEMOUND RD. P.O. BOX 13819 MILWAUKEE, WI 53213

Visit Hal Leonard Online at www.halleonard.com

Prices, contents & availability subject to change without notice.

0402

THE POP/ROCK ERA

Hal Leonard is proud to present these fantastic folios that gather the best popular songs from the '50s to today! All books arranged for piano, voice, and guitar.

THE POP/ROCK ERA: THE '50s

54 highlights from the first official decade of the pop/rock revolution, including: All Shook Up • At the Hop • Don't Be Cruel (To a Heart That's True) • Donna • Get a Job • Great Balls of Fire • Hound Dog • It's So Easy • Kansas City • (You've Got) Personality • That'll Be the Day • Why Do Fools Fall in Love • and more.
00310788..$14.95

THE POP/ROCK ERA: THE '60s

52 songs that helped shape the pop/rock era, including: Baby Love • Can't Take My Eyes off of You • Crying • Fun, Fun, Fun • Hey Jude • I Heard It Through the Grapevine • I Think We're Alone Now • Louie, Louie • Mony, Mony • Respect • Stand by Me • Stop! In the Name of Love • Wooly Bully • and more.
00310789..$14.95

THE POP/ROCK ERA: THE '70s

44 of the top songs from the '70s, including: ABC • Baby, I Love Your Way • Bohemian Rhapsody • Don't Cry Out Loud • Fire and Rain • I Love the Night Life • Imagine • Joy to the World • Just My Imagination (Running Away with Me) • The Logical Song • Oye Como Va • Piano Man • Three Times a Lady • We've Only Just Begun • You Are So Beautiful • and more.
00310790..$14.95

THE POP/ROCK ERA: THE '80s

38 top pop hits from the '80s, including: Back in the High Life Again • Centerfold • Every Breath You Take • Eye in the Sky • Higher Love •Summer of '69 • Sweet Dreams (Are Made of This) • Thriller • Time After Time • and more.
0031079..$14.95

THE POP/ROCK ERA: THE '90s

35 hits that shaped pop music in the 1990s, including: All I Wanna Do • Angel • Come to My Window • (Everything I Do) I Do It for You • Fields of Gold • From a Distance • Hard to Handle • Hero • I Will Remember You • Mambo No. 5 (A Little Bit Of...) • My Heart Will Go On (Love Theme from 'Titanic') • Ray of Light • Tears in Heaven • When She Cries • and more.
00310792..$14.95

Prices, contents and availability subject to change without notice.